Fast-Food Sonnets

poems

D1301738

Dennis Etzel Jr.

cover art by Aldrick Scott

Fast-Food Sonnets
poems by Dennis Etzel, Jr.

Edited by Brian Daldorph, Coal City Review, English Department,
University of Kansas, KS 66045

Layout by Pam LeRow, Institute for Digital Research in the
Humanities, University of Kansas

Printed by Lightning Source

briandal@ku.edu

ISBN-13

978-0-9795844-9-7

ISBN-10

0-9795844-9-3

1st printing, August 2016
2nd printing, September 2016

Acknowledgements

With thanks to the following editors:

Brian Daldorph of *Coal City Review*:
"Working Drive-Thru," "Small Fry," "Closing the Store on Summer Nights," "Buddy," "T-Bone," and "To Charlie Brown"

Amy Fleury of *Inscape*:
"The Poet-Cook"

Matt Porubsky of *seveneightfive*:
"Cleaning the Flat Grill," "Being Fired," and "From the Index to the Manager's Manual"

Mickey Cesar and Katie Longofono of *Blue Island Review*:
"Burning in the Lake of Fryer," "Dressing the Cheeseburger Buns," and "Waste"

Katie Longofono and Mary Stone of *Blue Island Review*:
"Birdy the Early Bird" and "Grimace"

Kevin Rabas of *Flint Hills Review*:
"Camouflage" and "Toying"

Table of Contents

III Characters

IV Fast Culture

V Exit Only

Introduction

The McDonald's I used to go to in Seattle was managed by a remarkable guy. He seemed to be the hub around which the entire restaurant revolved. Standing at the cash register in his short-sleeved dress shirt and floral tie, he directed the flow of traffic in the kitchen, at the drive-thru window, and in the dining area, simultaneously giving and taking orders throughout the day. He rarely smiled, but he never seemed brusque or harried—only superhumanly efficient. He'd politely ask for my order, his fingers would dance across the keypad, and in 45 seconds I'd be eating. I once saw him greet an older customer, notice her accent, and shift seamlessly into fluent Spanish. When he was on the clock, it seemed to me, his whole brilliant being was employed in the service of service.

I often wondered about this man's interior life. Did he excel in this job because he loved it, or in spite of the fact that he hated it? Was he grateful for it or resentful of it, or both? Did he go home and dream about it? What kind of dreams? Did he dream of doing something else eventually, or tomorrow? When he looked out the window on his morning bus ride and saw the University of Washington and the big hospitals and the commuters bound for Boeing and Microsoft and Amazon, how did he feel, knowing that his gifts would again be spent making fast food even faster?

A lot of poets have worked in chain restaurants. According to the company's own estimates, *one in eight American workers* will at some point pull a shift at McDonald's. But I've never seen anyone write about the experience with as much familiarity, immediacy, empathy, and insight as Dennis Etzel Jr. He has witnessed the thousand ways in which huge, impersonal bucket-wheel excavators of profit like McDonald's dehumanize their employees—not by failing to value them, but by reducing them to a specific set of valuable qualities: their energy, their availability, their malleability, and their willingness to work long hours for low pay (which is to say, their desperation). And because of his eye for the damning detail, his readers become witnesses, too: "A cook who had worked in the packing house // vouched for how machines removed those small bone / fragments out of the ground carcass and head. / Like added fillers, I felt absorbed in / the store's atmosphere. Like those cow eyeballs, / I could see myself blended in ..."

Yet *Fast-Food Sonnets* is finally a book about insuppressible humanity. Every poem documents some subversion of the corporate order, some assertion of individuality, some tiny victory of the imagination. Employees do a late-night solidarity dance in the parking lot, or re-imagine punitive fryer duty as a day at the beach: "Think of how the sun feels outside, compared / to the heat lamps reflecting off the back / mirror. How the beach feels, as salt gets stuck / under your nails with the frying oil. / People come in and check you out, looking / hot in your uniform ..." Co-workers steal meat for a cook-out, steal privacy in the stockroom, steal moments of peace after drive-thru traffic has died down "at night, quiet, and you can lean out / with the window open, into / the cool wind—" An ex-employee describes stealing time with his young children in the indoor play area, "evad[ing] the extremes, heat or cold, / dodging cashier's eyes as we do not buy."

The most impressive theft, though, is Etzel Jr.'s reclaiming of food-service life and language for poetry's purposes. At its essence, fast food is an infinitely reproducible simulacrum of naturalness— something these sonnets not only explore but embody. Their decasyllabic lines offer the appearance of meter without the music; their symmetry is as artificial as a Filet-O-Fish's. Many of them rebel against their own rectangularity, too, expanding or dwindling unexpectedly, or quitting mid-line with the relief of a cashier shucking off his uniform. And the sonnet is just one of the forms Etzel Jr. employs on his own terms. In a series of erasure poems, he exposes the insidious subtext of handbook-speak. "from the index to the Manager's Manual" is one of the most effective found poems I've ever read, a devastating indictment:

scripted responses, 232-242
>   to customer, 233-34; to employees,
>   234-36; to the media, 236-37; to
>   your family, 237-240

Etzel Jr. is delightfully alert to the little ironies in the air around him— the ways in which our words give us away: "meals named happy." Language seeks efficiency as ruthlessly as any corporate manager, and co-workers seek the camaraderie implicit in slang and shorthand.

Thus, in the most inorganic of environments, someone is always yelling "the need for a chef / or a side, a garden or a chicken."

"When I had no roof I made / Audacity my roof," Robert Pinsky writes in "Samurai Song." "When I had / No supper my eyes dined." When Dennis Etzel Jr. has no garden, he makes elision his garden. He has grown an orchard from concrete, and these poems are its windfall.

Eric McHenry
Poet Laureate of Kansas 2015-17 and author of *Odd Evening*

for the past, present, and future fast-food employees
who deserve more
and those who continue to fight
for change

Invocation

O Sing, Ronald! Clown with oversized hips,
painted smile and floppy shoes that don't fit
through doors that continue to easily
close. O Sing of your friends, the boy who takes
after his father the 'burgler—steal words!
Call on the mayor of verse, with his head
like a cheeseburger. Out, purple monster,
named after his grimace, scare them witless

into a mixed bag, to go. I write, sit
on a plastic bench. Come close. I listen
for your whisper, like static through drive-thru
speakers—the strain of years I dig under.
Evoke the name of Ray, a song to task,
to sing out from a styrofoam casket.

I

Beginnings

The Poet-Cook

Yes, that is my head peeking
    above the back counter,
that boy with wide eyes
    grinning in his third month
of flipping burgers and you,
    the poet-customer,
off. I know what the cow says
    when he's cold
flat on the grill, what the chickens
    say shuffling around
at three-hundred fifty degrees,
    while fish filets swim
up the stream of a boiling vat.
    I know the things
you don't get to see and hear,
    and I know your poems
with your black turtleneck and beret
    coffeehouse ensemble
don't hold up to the terrors
    of a polyester uniform.
What can you write about that?
    You unwrap the hamburger
for its mystery, unravel the French fry
    from its box. Remember
who put it there, who the witness is.
    You wish there was more
for you to write.

Interview

Have you ever worked fast food? Do you see
yourself as a clean worker? Do you have
a history? Do you hold grudges, tight?
Would you be available at the drop
of a phone call? Are you available
to work day through night? Would you be willing
to work eighty hours a week? Or eight?
Do you see yourself as a manager

someday? Today? Could you see
conducting an interview
like this? Does tomorrow
work for you, for interviewing
others? For coming in with this
inquisitive approach, this fresh uniform?

My First Day

working fast food, my first job, just two days
after my sixteenth birthday, and two months
of waiting to hear back from them after
I lied on my application that I
was sixteen at the time because I knew
they didn't hire anyone younger.
At sixteen, I needed this job, any
job, if I were to drive the Toyota

Tercel all the relatives helped to buy.
Mom said so. I'm in this picture without
a smile. She wanted to capture this time
of me at sixteen, ready to enter
the grown-up world. Sixteen, leaving home on
one last bicycle ride.

Camouflage

The first thing I did was to slip it on—
the blue polyester with white highlights
and tag with my name penciled in, beside
the arches. There is a photo of me
on the front porch, before I was sent off
to do my job. I have my visor pulled
over, almost hiding my eyes. I wished
not to be seen, out of fear of what men
might shout at me, tell me that I ruined things.
I wondered why I was going, why I
even signed up. Alongside the veterans—
the employees who served time as alone
as I was—we each did the job well, while
knowing we didn't make a difference.

Training Videos

Watch them in the break room while on the clock.
Learn how to smile like the actors, as one
suggests to a customer, *Apple pies*
and cookies make nice desserts, included
at an inexpensive price. Managers
watch their own films, learn their lines when speaking
to employees. *Is everything okay?*
the male manager asks the new, young girl.
I noticed you are not as productive,
he says with concern, assures her he's there
and he cares. *The restaurant is like home,*
with a kitchen and dining room our guests
fill. He talks about employee appearance,
to wear her hair up, be ready to serve.

You Are

now a temporary job. You might
welcome a tool to use throughout
job functions in the workplace.
Additional resources. The sole purpose
is to guide you in need, not to solve
a problem. Additional resources are
you, we hope. Manual.

Schedules

You start with an availability
that switches to when you are needed
to work other hours. Day
becomes night, then back,
as sleep is your only rest
until you work again. And again,
they change the lines
that mark one hour to another.
They call to say you are late.
You will also work longer that day.
They give you a Monday
off, then a Wednesday,
so Tuesday is a torture, a reminder
of how bad the weekend ended.
Sometimes they call on these days
off to tell you they need you
to come in. You feel wanted,
like you belong.

An Employee

must not draw any attention
when on duty. Not permitted.
Is not allowed.

II

Stations

Working Drive-Thru

The idea starts with a window turned
racetrack, a way to drive up to exchange
money for food. Now we use computer
screens, headsets, cameras—technology
to say hello, punch in the order, say
please pull around, which means to promptly move
into the merging lane, as everyone
hunts and gathers this way. The idea
turned to impatience, everywhere, people
wanting service—now. Sometimes the line dies
down at night, quiet, and you can lean out
with the window open, into
the cool wind—

Making Salads

Drive-thru always yells the need for a chef
or a side, a garden or a chicken.
On the farm where the packaged lettuce grew,
just by the barn's north side, there are chickens
free to roam in the garden, not inside
those alleged caged prisons. A chef surveys
the soil's fertile texture. On afternoons
at two, a man in a red uniform
made of polyester sweeps everything
into his arms—lettuce, carrots, chickens,
hogs. Loads a truck bound for a factory
where each thing naturally falls asleep,
passes away to a painless dicer
or chopper. From conveyer belt into
cardboard boxes, loaded on truck again,
and sent to this restaurant, this salad-
making table of stainless steel under
flickers of fluorescent, no drop of red
evident on either plastic-gloved hand.

Stock Room

You fetch wrappers or stacks of cups and lids,
whatever needs refilled. The dry products,
they call them—napkins, sauces, boxes, straws,
and all of the containers to place food inside.
You slip into the back for wandering,
full of worry, wishing to pour coffee
from out of your buzzing body. Timers
sound like managers—beep for attention—
and you come here to get away. Sometimes
managers' voices are sirens, warnings
to take cover. You find empty boxes
in that room, that you were told to smash down,
recycle, but you keep them as places
to hide. These boxes can seat up to five.

Basic Job Functions of Each Worker

Position a basic understanding of an order.
Welcome to your order! Take the order
(asking, *Anything else? Will that be all?)*
Ordering, their order is correct. Read
their order as in the picture shown.
Their order is correct. Important to
their order: say, *Thank You.*

Small Fry

As punishment after being called out
as lazy, you are placed on the station
for bagging French fries, knowing anyone
can pick up the handle, place containers
on the end, and with a flip of the wrist,
send the scooped fries falling down off the pile.
Think of how the sun feels outside, compared
to the heat lamps reflecting off the back
mirror. How the beach feels, as salt gets stuck
under your nails with the frying oil.
People come in and check you out, looking
hot in your uniform, as if glowing
from the fluorescent rays, with the power
to make many servings just by request.

Cleaning the Flat Grill

I scrape the carbon off of the flat grill,
as another member from the kitchen
is off—let go—after the manager
yells at him, tells him to mop the back room
before leaving. The grill scraper is sharp—
takes off the brown ashes. The manager
jokes with me about something, as a way
to let the boy know he is not wanted.

I push down hard to get the residue
off the metal, wishing for smooth silver
again. The manager turns his back on
that young man he laughs at. I do my best—
to nod, smile, continue to scrape away
any hope for this surface to be clean.

Dressing the Cheeseburger Buns

As toasted buns report like young soldiers
onto the dressing table, a timer
of the mind begins—to break the clinging
hearts apart and place each condiment on
tops before the burgers drop. I was taught
the uniform of these dressings—one squeeze
from the mustard and ketchup guns, pickle
with onions that fit the size of quarters—

but I wished to do more, to throw grenades
of extra pickles and cheese on, to give
to the boy who wants a happiness meal.
But the order was in—to keep my head
down and do the work I was told to do,
without a question of what we fight for.

For Each Specific Job Will Be Uniform

A tag, your own.
Limited leg on
the seams. Arm-up
running. You may not
come in. You are not
completely in.

Burning in the Lake of Fryer

Potatoes, cows, fish, and chickens—the list
of the condemned will soon include you, how
you are cut down and frozen while at work
in the kitchen, a deer caught in the flash
of finished timers—the sign of failure—
even when you follow the manual
as the word, as a devout employee,
the manager brings down fryer baskets

shaped like iron fists and ends illusions
of meals named happy, and you feel like these
things you load into the wired cages—
pushed, shipped, mangled, spliced, reshaped, and lowered
lower than your visor can look downward
into the fryer that endlessly burns.

Grease

on the spatulas, the hands, all fingers
burned from touching the cooked meat, the smell of
burnt hamburger left on the grill to scrape
into the grease trap full of the day's ooze.
The question was: who *would* get stuck with that
car door full of grease, and steer it outside
for disposal, holding onto the warm
encasing as the swamp sloshed back and forth?

In winter, from the back door through the lot,
success steadily crept as steam climbed high
to join the breath. One time, someone did slip.
He worked two hours in the cold to scoop
up the layer that never fully froze.
As spring came, that dark reminder remained.

Conventional

They say the special ovens will arrive
to replace everything you know about
keeping food fresh. Why not call these little
cookers literally—as microwaves?
This is not the job you trained for—how meat
comes off the grill, onto the bun and up
to the heating lamps, and wrapped right away,
placed into hot bins the temperature
of the sun. Forget everything you know.
There is no questioning authority,
no procedure for protest. Everyone
will be retrained, resent into the field
while the ovens are coming in, landing
by parachute—foreign territory.

Only Duty

You did not receive any family and friends
when coming to request, to disturb working.

Doing Truck

Slang is slung around side to side
in the five-o'clock-in-the-morning manner
after the outside door to the walk-in freezer
opens. The cold comes out as fog
onto the truck's back where we unload
and open boxes, pulling out goodies
like thieves. Managers like me supervised
inventory coming in, so nothing

slipped back out. After cases of burgers
went missing, the joke was: Kenny would have
a barbeque. I understood why some
would steal. Even as I earned a couple
dollars over minimum wage, days off
sometimes meant going cold hungry.

Process

After the delivery truck driver
hinted that we didn't want to know how
corporate defines what beef is, our eyes
examined each pink, frozen, shaped patty
and reports further. After the slaughter
and slicing, it made sense, that everything
remaining was set aside for this place.
A cook who had worked in a packing house

vouched for how machines removed those small bone
fragments out of the ground carcass and head.
Like added fillers, I felt absorbed in
the store's atmosphere. Like those cow eyeballs,
I could see myself blended in, from rare
to well done on the grill.

Waste

is what we label food after holding
past a certain time. *Our food expires,*
we are told when hired, and learn compound
words, like wastecount, wastebucket, while we watch
each sandwich thrown away into buckets,
counted in the back, each still warm and wrapped.
One time, Steve snagged seven cheeseburgers out,
went to the break room and ate them, to show
he would survive. After close, everything
is waste—pies and salads even counted.
We sometimes include ranch dressing, knowing
leftovers will be gone by the morning.

Closing the Store on Summer Nights

The closing hour turns to cleaning, turns to
leaving at two in the morning, as night
employees stretch out on the grass, beside
their parked cars, as the automatic lights
shut off, like they are told to do, commands
given by the manager. Each face turns
to the stars, those wishes to find a way
out of this job. The hands that touched burgers
to wrap in wrappers, fixed cold drinks, now smell
of grease and French fries, now dig to replace
these gross scents with grass and flower petals,
fingers pushing deeper into the earth.

III

Characters

Westown

we called it, our ol' fast-food restaurant
known as West-town, but dropped a "t" to mock
our boss' name. His best years were taking
orders in the Navy. Now he would give
them out. He would say, *Sir? Sir? I work for
a living.* One time I bottlenecked, he
said, the term used incorrectly. Food was
not ready in time, somehow my fault, but

I wasn't going to say the bottleneck
was him. Instead, I cleaned the walls, bathroom
doors, as a kind of humiliating
punishment. Twenty years later, he still
walks around that store late at night, with broom,
dustpan, and bag, cleaning the lot, head high.

The Proper Process

for documenting a complaint: you
want to file a complaint ensuring
that. You are closing. Complete
and store safe your system to
document the day.

Trade-Off

Leslie, the store manager, knew how to
bribe me when we received a promotion
for films—fantasy or science fiction.
She bartered with me: the life-sized standup
of Michael Keaton, as Batman Returns,
for help in scrubbing down the parking lot.
From midnight to four, we poured degreaser
onto motor oil stains and other spots,

then with water and brushes cleaned the whole
lot up. When our Gotham City fell dead
to silence, I realized why being
alone out here could be scary. We don't
live in the town of a Bruce Wayne, but armed
with our quickness we were sidekicks, the same.

Buddy

He loved the spotlight, dancing as he trained
us on how to fry burgers. But he knew
his fast life would outrun this fast food life
some day. *I have to get out to run
a mission*, he would say. Even the cooks on
work-release from jail didn't take him
seriously, yelling, *Yeah, Buddy!*
It was code for "nonsense," for all the dreams

of making it rich that sizzled away.
One night, squad cars splashed reds and blues to drown
the lot, as a police spotlight found him
getting into the getaway
car—his. The drive-thru cashier straight up asked,
Does this mean he won't be in for his shift?

T-Bone

The first black man I ever met who knew
Led Zepplin from Motley Crue. *Have a new
old lady*, he said. I met her after
work when we all went for drinks at The Club
Paradise. A cashier I liked was there
too, but for a manager it's taboo.
*I'm telling you, Jazz on the radio
is nothing like Blues in Kansas City,*

T-Bone said that night. His lady agreed.
We planned to go on a trip to KC
together. Get away. Maybe check out
the Royals. We made plans to the tunes
of "Love Stinks" and "Sweet Dreams." We danced around
the parking lot as though we believed.

To Charlie Brown

Also the name of the cook stabbed to death
with a butter knife by his girlfriend.
We found out when he didn't come to work.
He was comical. He hid his problems:
one was his mind; two, this fast food job;
the third I learned just three days prior.
I found him outside the walk-in freezer
frozen, in shock. He explained how he fled

on foot through the snow from robbers one time
during his Army gig in Alaska.
The thieves took his clothes and jeep, so he ran
back to base numb, almost dying.
After that, he hated the cold. Hated
working in that room, alone.

Gary

was homeless
when I hired him,
his girlfriend's address
on the application. He now
gets his meals "to go,"
takes to his new apartment
any thrown out
empty boxes.

They are like the ones I wept in,
I mishear, followed
by how stealing stereos
is a more honest job
than these bosses' jobs. I can feel
my hours here stolen.

Pay Day

That day falls.
Payout will not,
does not permit
advance. Men
will evaluate
your rate of pay
and, therefore, remove
your status.

Being Fired

Like magic, an employee turns
sharp corners of counters
to vanish,

resembles a manager's hand folding
an employee's used uniform
over

like a handkerchief, as her body
that inhabited those clothes is gone
with a wave of his hand,

goodbye, makes the comment,
We will never see her
again, as if uttering magic words

found on the side
of a children's meal box,
and like a true magician, holds

onto the secret of how
he made her
disappear.

Grimace

Before they turn the cameras on
for the commercial, they shove
a shake into my hand
and say, "You know what to do"
again, in that sing-song way.
It took me a while to look up the definition
for "condescending," like when a woman
asked me, "How can you let them be so condescending?"
It's part of the gig. "Be purple," they say,
"Dance around and laugh,
stupid." I remember a time
when I was actually happy. Now I play
the part—silly and dumb.
Sometimes I forget when cameras are off.

Birdie the Early Bird

They want me because of that part about getting
the worm, that my name implies a breakfast
mascot as it has "early" in it
but I'm not. I like to sleep
in, not set the alarm
that sounds like a buzzer
for the hash browns or to say
it's time to remove the scrambled eggs from the grill.

Yes, the manager yells
at me for being late,
but I just let it ricochet,
wing it off. They make me wear
these fake feathers.
I can't fly.

IV

Fast Culture

That Nostalgia

Yes, I miss the days of McDonaldland
cookies and McDLTs, when the hot
side's hot and the cold side's cold. We knew what
to expect then. Ordering was simple.
The value meal really was a value
for less than three dollars because we were
in a recession. *Two all-beef patties,*
special sauce, lettuce, geez, sometimes I wish

I could get a box of shortbread cookies
in the shapes of characters, a Shamrock
Shake that is only vanilla with green
dye, not flavored with mint. It's lucky to
think back on these things, pulling out the toy
we each want out of this box we carry.

The Rib Sandwich

is back. This Fall. Is frozen first, each shape
and size equal, then shipped in a cardboard
sarcophagus to restaurants. Is cooked,
is coated with barbeque, is placed in
a bun made with pinches of chemicals
like azodicarbonamide, for bleached
flour, for gym mats and the soles of shoes.
Is found with The Rib locator websites,

twitter accounts, and the smell of pig parts
like tripe, heart, and scalded stomach, blended
with salt water to bind them together.
Is the appearance of a rib without
any rib meat inside. Salt will preserve,
so The Rib rises to outlive us all.

The Game with Money

When the first promotion began,
when the game pieces
were loose and employees
started playing,
it was easy to put those chances
in your pocket
when no one was watching. Yes,
everyone stole them like it was Wall Street.

Who couldn't turn
down the chance to win a million
or an order of fries? The mustached
man in the top hat
sat on mounds of money
while eating a Big Burger.

From the Index to the Manager's Manual

Toying

Barbie or Hot Wheels? I ask the mother
when she orders a Happy Meal for her son.
Many employees call the Barbies girl toys
as Hot Wheels are for boys. I argue
a boy might want a doll
and a girl might dream of racing someday.
The store manager allowed me to change
the buttons, reprogram the registers
that said BOY TOY and GIRL TOY. However,
the customer yells at me, *How dare you
imply my son would want a Barbie toy.*
I stand looking just as confused, upset,
holding the toys, one in each hand
as if they need balancing, an act.

Playland

I never thought I'd be happy to see
a McDonald's in my life, Carrie says,
building excitement about the rebuilt
store close to home, complete with a playland.
We know how they manipulate children
and parents with their "Happy Meal," now with
healthier choices. What child really wants
McApples, though? But now we have children
find the playlands to be winter havens,

except for Topeka Boulevard's, where
a fight between parents broke out during
a kid's party. But this one is in North
Topeka where only North Topekans
go. We'll evade the extremes, heat or cold,
dodging cashier's eyes as we do not buy.

Fast-Food Birthday Party

I saw the red of taillights, then the man,
the drive-thru customer reports after
the police arrive. Someone verifies
the suspect was busy texting someone.
The lull stagnates into a sharp silence.
Someone shouts from the men's restroom—to jump
out hollering about how his one boy's
grandmother ruined the birthday party.
Where is the boy? someone asks. *The taillights
shined there, red*, the customer repeats.
Tonight, the moon turns red. Tonight, the man
will be caught in the parking lot. Will we
get back to when the drive thru was empty,
with the boy's wish in front of lit candles?

M**o**lds

It comes together for me when Jamie
Oliver demonstrates how he can grind
up a chicken carcass, squeeze the meat out
from the bone fragments, mix in additives
to mold into chicken nugget pieces.
After time in back we had the three shapes
memorized: round and rectangle white meat
with pieces of dark meat like Florida.

When the picture of the fried and battered
chicken head hit the papers, it did not
surprise me, how those things left over from
what is valued can be squeezed together,
reshaped, made pretty, while somewhere trauma
runs around in the backroom, unaware.

V

Exit Only

Fast-Food Restaurant Playset

After seeing the commercial on TV, I wanted one,
like other children on the block had one
complete with: workers and customers,
a lever to slide out trays full of food,
a cash register that rings, a merry-
go-round of merchandising.
Everything made
entirely of plastic:

brown building, brown and tan
tables, with pretend food
served by happy employees
eaten by happy people
with every smile
painted on.

Picture a New Fast-Food Location

Asmund worries there will be another
one of them built here, but it is only
a photo of the first one ever placed
in a book about their success, designed
for children grades three through seven. Yes, there
will be some ground breaking somewhere complete
with happy meals, balloons, Ronald himself.
All the children are told to shout his name.

Have birthday parties there. Get
kids in there. These plans manufactured
by the corporate office. Even have
white or chocolate cakes decorated
with fast-food characters,
candles blown out.

Caveat

You can reinjure yourself at the wrists
with the spatula on the grill, the twist
from dumping French fry baskets, on your arms
lifting the boxes of frozen eerie-
pink meat patties, on your feet by running
speedy-speed, shoving product into bags,
cleaning the parking lot, in your chest, in
your chest, all of these revisits to there,

the there of the fast food restaurant
of your mind can hurt as the body
remembers, as
the body remembers
years of aching
hands, knees—

Heavy

Through the tug of the door, the same old tug
when you first went through the door, the same scents
scientifically placed inside food as
aromas flood you when you step inside
the door. You can always go back, but get
stuck. The weight of belonging, the weight of
being part of the process, of open
doors. Recycled smells, employees, the warm

vent air pushed into all of our faces.
Feeling needed, even when treated
like trash. The trash can liners
are in the back if you ever
need to empty the full bins
and start filling up again.

Words of Thanks and Reflection

First, a big thanks to Brian Daldorph and Coal City Press. Brian, you always commented on how you loved the poems I sent you, and I appreciate your words, your presence, and your enthusiasm. Really, you are a big reason for why I continued working on these poems, hoping to get a book-length collection.

I have other people to thank, too, like the editors who published some of the poems in their literary journals: Kevin Rabas, Amy Fleury, Mickey Cesar, Katie Longofono, Mary Stone, and Matt Porubsky.

Also a big thanks to Aldrick Scott for the cover art.

I started on these poems back in 2002, finished in 2015, about a time of my life from 1986 through 1993. It was years in the making on both counts.

Eric Schlosser comments in his 2001 book *Fast Food Nation*, "Instead of relying upon a small, stable, well-paid, and well-trained workforce, the fast food industry seeks out part-time, unskilled workers who are willing to accept low pay. Teenagers have been the perfect candidates for these jobs, not only because they are less expensive to hire than adults, but also because their youthful inexperience makes them easier to control."

When I asked on Facebook how many poets ever worked fast food, the response was astonishing. I found out that Jon Tribble has a manuscript, too, about his experience working for KFC. I also learned Mark Nowak worked at Wendy's during the entire Reagan presidency (1980-1988). Also, Amy King worked at McDonald's for years. I did, too.

I certainly wanted these poems to speak to my formative years, to the epiphanies and heartbreaks of feeling trapped in a job. I do not want to make this collection political, but can't help but think of the work we still need to do. *Food, Inc., A Place at the Table, Super Size Me*, and all of the documentaries in both film and book form trying to point out the truth in a time of the need for overhauling all systems. Please also check out *Chew On This: Everything You Don't Want to Know About Fast Food*. The film *Fast Food Nation* is the fictional account of what is found in Eric Schlosser's book and worth viewing, too.

Workers' rights, the food industry, and big business: Will it take a reshifting of the hierarchy of power into a shared power? Can it be something healthy, local-based, self-sustaining, job-creating, and on the side of everyone's best interests?

About the Poet

Dennis Etzel Jr. lives with Carrie and the boys in Topeka, Kansas where he teaches English at Washburn University. He has an MFA from The University of Kansas, and an MA and Graduate Certificate in Women and Gender Studies from Kansas State University. His previous work includes two chapbooks, *The Sum of Two Mothers* (ELJ Publications 2013) and *My Graphic Novel* (Kattywompus Press 2015), and a full-length poetic memoir *My Secret Wars of 1984* (BlazeVOX 2015). His work has appeared in *Denver Quarterly, Indiana Review, BlazeVOX, Fact-Simile, 1913: a journal of poetic forms, 3:AM, Tarpaulin Sky, DIAGRAM*, and others. He is a TALK Scholar for the Kansas Humanities Council and leads poetry workshops in various Kansas spaces. Please feel free to connect with him at dennisetzeljr.com.

About the Artist

Aldrick Scott, in his own words: I was born on January 12, 1975 in Minneapolis, MN and later moved to Florida after a snowstorm. One of my dreams in life was to become a super hero, so I joined the Marine Corps right after high school in June of 1993. I served 10 years in the Marine Corps as a Embarkation Specialist. I created movement plans to deploy units for overseas training and combat deployments. I traveled to many countries and deployed to Iraq in 2003. In June of 2005, I left the Marine Corps and joined the United States Army as a Water Purification Specialist. I was responsible for transporting and purifying water from different sources to make it safe to drink. Some of my personal achievements include receiving my Air Assault badge when I was at Fort Campbell, Kentucky; as well as leading the Air Assault prep course for 101st Airborne Division, where I trained soldiers for their upcoming Air Assault slots. I have been to Iraq four times and received a Combat Action Badge on my first tour with the Army. While being at Fort Riley, Kansas, I received several certifications for combat and self-defense. I was the Battalion's Instructor and Sexual Assault and Rape Prevention representative for my unit. In my spare time, I did Mauy Thai and Brazilian Jiu Jitsu. While teaching and competing in tournaments, I placed first in an amateur division. I later became a Platoon Sergeant to eighty men and women. I am now 41 years old and retired from the military after serving twenty years. Currently, I am in my third year at Washburn University and continuing my Bachelor's degree in Fine Arts. I wish to eventually make a cartoon series one day. My passion is art and I hope to inspire everyone around me with my work. While at Washburn, I was awarded Student Artist of the Month in February 2016. I have had my art displayed at the Mulvane Art Museum and Downtown Topeka. My dreams of being an artist are made possible through the support of my wonderful woman and four children who are by my side through everything I do.

Please check out these other amazing Coal City Press titles:

Music I Once Could Dance To, by Roy J. Beckemeyer. A 2015 Kansas
    Notable Book.
Bird's Horn & Other Poems, by Kevin Rabas.
Sonny Kenner's Red Guitar, by Kevin Rabas.
Poem on the Range: A Poet Laureate's Love Song to Kansas, by Caryn
    Mirriam-Goldberg.

CPSIA information can be obtained
at www.ICGtesting.com
Printed in the USA
LVOW10s0851110318
569446LV00010B/635/P